Handheld G

CW01514213

Hello, my name is Eric Bowden and I have been gaming since the mid 1980's right up to the present day from Commodore 64 to Playstation 4.

I have been lucky enough to play thousands of games on dozens of machines and I have loved them all (except for the CDI of course), but for me the 1990's were the Golden Era of gaming from the Super Nintendo and Sega Megadrive to The Sony Playstation and Nintendo 64.

There was also a thriving Arcade Scene during this time with fantastic games from the likes of Sega, Namco and Capcom.

In this book I will look at another Gaming Sector that is often overlooked, Handheld Gaming (covering the 1990's and the 2000's), from The Original Nintendo Gameboy and Sega's Game Gear to The Gameboy Advance and Nintendo DS to Sony's PSP there was so much for gamers to enjoy here.

I will look at each Handheld Console and attempt to choose my 5 favourite games on each format and then another 5 addition Honourable Mentions. This should be lots of fun I hope you will join me, many thanks.

Nintendo Gameboy

The Nintendo Gameboy was released in April of 1989 in Japan followed by The North American Launch in July 1989 and then eventually onto Europe in late 1990. The Gameboy was Nintendo's first portable Console and was a real masterpiece of design, despite being rather limited Technically even for the time period with a Monochrome Screen the Gameboy would go on to sell well in excess of 115 Million units in total.

Despite rival Handheld Consoles offering full colour screens (such as Atari's Lynx and Sega's Game Gear) The Gameboy was able to offer a much bigger and better games library and crucially much better battery consumption, whereas The Sega Game Gear would burn through 6 AA batteries in less than 5 hours The Gameboy could last easily 20 hours on only 4 AA batteries.

Towards the end of the 1990's Nintendo released several revisions to the Gameboy Hardware namely The Gameboy Pocket (essentially a smaller model with even better battery consumption) and eventually The Gameboy Color which finally added colour graphics in addition to an even faster processor and more memory, battery consumption was improved further still to an incredible 30 hours).

The Gameboy Color was compatible with all the original Gameboy games as well as having a fantastic library all of it's own.

Over the course of its life The Original Gameboy had a games library of over 1000 titles which makes it really difficult to choose just 5 of my favourite and 5 more honourable mentions but I will give it my best shot.

Top 5 Gameboy Games

Super Mario Land 2: 6 Golden Coins

The original Super Mario Land was an excellent 2D Platformer for The Gameboy, before I played it I thought it would likely be just a watered down version of the classic Nes games but that was not the case at all.

Super Mario Land contained all the gaming goodness of the Home Console version but I would say with an increased focus on puzzle solving (I also really liked the Egyptian theme of the earlier levels).

The game was very popular and sold extremely well and so with this in mind a sequel was somewhat inevitable and so it proved. Released in early 1993 in Europe Super Mario Land 2: 6 Golden Coins managed to improve still further on its excellent predecessor.

The improvements included making the game much larger, indeed there are 6 huge worlds to conquer here before Mario eventually reaches the 7th world and has to do battle with the evil Wario (I believe this was Wario's first ever appearance).

Graphically the game has been improved over the original game with much larger sprites and more detailed backdrops. The sound has also been upgraded from the first game and was composed by the now legendary videogame composer Kazumi Totaka.

Super Mario Land 2: 6 Golden Coins was very popular with gamers and critics alike and went on to sell well over 10 million copies. Infact so popular was this game that it was rereleased on Nintendo Switch in early 2023 making it easily accessible to a whole new audience.

Donkey Kong 94

Released in Europe in September 1994 Donkey Kong 94 was a superb sequel to the 1980's Arcade Classic Donkey Kong.

The opening few levels are classic Donkey Kong Arcade with Super Mario having to reach the top of the level in order to save the lovely 'Pauline' from the clutches of the big Ape. But soon the gameplay style shifts greatly to include far more puzzle solving elements as Super Mario must again rescue Pauline from Donkey Kong.

Super Mario has to work his way through a mammoth 101 levels spread over 10 different stages each one more difficult than the last.

Graphically the game was superb especially if played via The Super Gameboy on The Super Nintendo which added a limited colour palette which really helped to bring the game to life.

I would recommend Donkey Kong 64 to any Gameboy owners especially fans of Super Mario or platform or puzzle based titles.

So popular was this game that it was later released on Nintendo's 3DS Console in 2011, hopefully it will be added onto Nintendo Switch at some stage in the future.

Tetris

How Could I not talk about Tetris when looking at my favourite Gameboy games? Created by Alexey Pajitnov in the mid 1980's and released on a variety of platforms including most famously The Nintendo Gameboy.

Tetris is for me the most playable and addictive puzzle games ever devised and was the perfect game to showcase The Gameboy. Although Home versions of Tetris would later add better graphics and extra game modes The Gameboy version is sheer joy with clear and simple graphics, a very responsive and easy to use control system and some of the best music on the legendary Handheld Console.

The gameplay is very simple various blocks of differing sizes and shapes (called Tetrominoes) come down the screen with the player having to use the different pieces to create Horizontal lines, when the player has completed a line it will disappear with the pieces above it falling down a level. The player will be rewarded for this achievement with points which will eventually result in the difficulty increasing until even the most skilled player will be overwhelmed with the speed of the falling pieces and its Game Over.

Tetris was a huge success at the time with the game eventually going on to sell well over 35 million copies although sadly the designer Alexey Pajitnov actually received almost no royalties from the sales of the game as under the Soviet Dictatorship of the time most of the profits went straight to the Soviet Government via a company called ELORG.

If you own a Gameboy you simply must try this game it is probably the most addictive game on the entire platform!

The Legend of Zelda: Link's Awakening

Usually I am not really a big fan of RPG's (Role Playing Games) but that being said I have always enjoyed The Legend of Zelda series including this one Link's Awakening.

Just like the majority of the other games in this series Link's Awakening is an action-adventure game featuring equal parts combat and exploration.

The story here involves Link traveling to different countries in order to obtain new skills to tackle future threats to Hyrule, however due to a storm Link's ship is destroyed and in order to return home he must find The Wind Fish (we have all been there).

Link's Awakening actually introduced several new gameplay mechanics to the series including special trading sequences, mini boss battles and even playing music via an Ocarina. These fresh gameplay additions really helped to elevate the game over many of its rivals and as a result the game still stands up to this very day.

Such was the huge popularity of this game that it was rereleased on The Gameboy Colour in late 1998, this version officially called The Legend of Zelda: Link's Awakening DX made several improvements to the game including full colour graphics as well as an extra dungeon. This version of the game is now available to play via The Nintendo Switch, even if you are not a fan of this genre you must try this game as it may just change your mind.

Kirby's Dreamland

Released in late 1992 in Europe Kirby's Dreamland was an exceptional platformer starring the now legendary 'Pink Puff'.

Kirby has to help the good folk of Dream Land fight off the evil King Dedede who has stolen all of their food (bit rude).

The gameplay is your standard 2d platforming involving Kirby overcoming various enemies and obstacles in order to reach the end of each level. Kirby has several special abilities to aid him on his quest including the ability to fly and even to inhale a great many of his enemies.

Kirby's Dreamland features various interesting boss fights throughout the game including the evil dictator King Dedede and Whispy Woods (who is a giant tree and king of the forest).

The game was very popular upon its release and several sequels were made for The Nintendo Gameboy but for me this title was always my personal favourite.

The game has since been rereleased on The Virtual Console on The Nintendo 3DS and later on The Wii via Kirby's Dream Collection, it was later made available on Nintendo Switch as part of The Nintendo Switch Online service. If you are a fan of 2d platform games you must try this game you will no be disappointed.

Honourable Mentions

Mortal Kombat 2

For the most part Beat Em Up's do not usually work very well on Handheld platforms such as Nintendo's Gameboy but Mortal Kombat 2 is an exception to the rule.

Sure the game cannot compete with the Home Console versions of Mortal Kombat 2 due to the small screen and lack of available buttons but despite this the game still manages to pack an almighty punch.

There are a total of 8 fighters to choose from (including the evil shape shifter Shang Tsung), each fighter still has their very own finishing moves called fatalities. The controls whilst scaled back from the 16 bit versions of Mortal Kombat 2 still work very well and most importantly are very responsive.

Graphically the game is much better than it has any right to be with well detailed and animated sprites and surprisingly good backdrops.

All in all I believe Mortal Kombat 2 to be the very best game from this genre on The Gameboy, if you enjoy fighting games you must give this game a try just don't compare It to the Home versions or indeed the Arcade Cabinet.

Super R.C Pro-AM

Racing games on handheld machines are often rather disappointing but Super R.C Pro -AM is different, based on the classic Nes game R.C Pro-AM this title has much to offer.

Graphically the game was awesome considering the available hardware, viewed from an isometric angle the car sprites are clear and pretty detailed whilst the tracks are both interesting and easy to navigate.

The controls are simple but very responsive and unlike many other games from this genre Super R.C Pro-AM offers a career mode of sorts involving the player attempting to finish in the top 3 positions for each race, if successful the next track will be unlocked until eventually all 24 tracks are available.

The game also offers weapons to use on rival vehicles and various speed boost items as well, whilst this game will likely never be as widely respected as its Nes counterpart it still has much to offer fans of racing titles.

R Type

Released on Gameboy in 1991 R Type was a superb scrolling shoot em up that whilst not in the same league as its Arcade or Home Console counterparts still has much to recommend it.

As with most other games from this genre the premise is simple kill or be killed and in that regard this game really delivers!

Graphically the game is as good as it possibly could have been bearing in mind the limitations of the Console, the screen scrolls both quickly and smoothly with very little slowdown even when loads of enemies are on screen.

The controls work extremely well with little or no input lag and the soundtrack considering its on Gameboy was more than respectable.

The only downside is that in order to fit the game onto a Handheld Console several enemy types and a few levels had to be removed but that aside this is still a great shooter.

Mega Man 5

Released during November 1994 in Europe Mega Man 5 was an amazing action platformer featuring the affable Mega Man in his eternal struggle against the evil Dr Wily and his evil army of robots.

The majority of the gameplay involves Mega Man using various weapons (mainly his arm cannon) to clear each stage of baddies before eventually taking on and defeating a huge robot boss in order to progress to the next level.

Just like all of the other games in this series the difficulty level is somewhat harsh but with practice the game can be conquered.

Although Mega Man 5 does not quite match the brilliance of the various Home Console equivalents it still has much to offer fans of the genre.

In 2013 Mega Man 5 was released on the Virtual Console for The Nintendo 3DS so that a new generation of gamers could appreciate its charms.

Castlevania 2: Belmont's Revenge

Known as Dracula Densetsu 2 in Japan Castlevania 2: Belmont's Revenge was an action platformer released in late 1992 in Europe.

The plot here involves Christopher Belmont taking on the evil Dracula who has kidnaped his son Soleil and turned him into a demon (we have all been there).

There are 4 massive levels for the player to complete and unlike many other titles in this genre the player can actually choose the order he or she tackles each level in.

Unlike earlier games in the series here Christopher Belmont can use sub weapons (a cross and some holy water), this helps greatly as each level is jam packed with powerful enemies.

A great many people regard this game as the best in the series on Handheld and to be honest I am one of them, if you are a fan of this genre or this series you simply must try this game.

Castlevania 2: Belmont's Revenge was later released alongside several other classic Konami titles (including the amazing shooter Gradius 2) on Konami GB Collection Volume 4 on The Gameboy Color in 2000.

Sega Game Gear

Released in 1990 in Japan and the following year in both Europe and North America The Game Gear was a handheld Console that unlike The Gameboy included a full colour backlit screen.

The hardware inside the Game Gear was very impressive for the time to the extent that many people viewed it as a portable Sega Master System (as a result it would receive a great many high quality conversions from said Home Console).

The downside of this of course was that as a result The Game Gear never really ended up getting many exclusives and without any must play games of it own it sadly was not able to compete against the almighty Gameboy.

Another huge problem with The Game Gear was the extremely poor battery life, whereas a Gameboy could go for over 15 hours on 4 AA batteries the poor old Game Gear could only manage around 3 hours on 6 AA batteries. This really killed the machine stone dead as a viable option for handheld gamers and as a result The Console only went on to sell around 10 million units worldwide.

Despite the many drawbacks I have fond memories of The Game Gear and I enjoyed many a happy hour playing on it (although I only really played it at home plugged into the mains due to the poor battery life) and despite the games library being no were near the size of The Gameboy library it still had over 350 games and I will now cover my favourites.

Top 5 Game Gear Games

Sonic The Hedgehog

I have always been a huge fan of The Megadrive Sonic games and so with that in mind I was really looking forward to playing Sonic The Hedgehog on Game Gear.

I was not disappointed! Of course Sonic on Game Gear cannot quite compete with the Megadrive version but still it has much to offer (it was largely based on The Master System version).

The graphics are among the very best that the Console has to offer with bright, colourful and detailed sprites and backdrops, the sound was surprisingly good as well with some very catchy tunes and the controls are both simple and very responsive too.

All six zones from The Megadrive version are included here and the gameplay is still classic Sonic!

The only negative and to be fair it is only to be expected given the limitations of the Hardware is the lack of speed compared to the 16 bit original, that's not to say that Sonic on Game Gear is not fast but not quite as fast as The Megadrive games.

That aside Sonic The Hedgehog on Game Gear is still a fantastic platform game and is a must own if you are a fan of the blue blur!

Road Rash

Released in early 1994 Road Rash on The Game Gear was a vehicular combat game based on the classic Mega Drive game of the same name.

Although not in the same league as its Mega Drive counterpart Road Rash on the Game Gear is still a class act.

Graphically the game was excellent with large sprites and very impressive detail and scrolling effects on each track, the animations were also very smooth with little or no slowdown or screen tearing.

The sound effects are much better than you might expect for a handheld racing game and most importantly the gameplay is still solid gold (involving the player attempting to win various races whilst avoiding obstacles and fighting against rival bikers).

In my opinion Road Rash on Game Gear is probably the very best racing game available on the Console and is a must buy if you are a fan of the genre.

Streets of Rage 2

Streets of Rage 2 is yet another Mega Drive conversion (see a pattern emerging here) but a very good one all the same.

The Mega Drive game is arguably the best game available on that Console and the same is true with this version.

The graphics are very nearly the same as the Mega Drive game with superb sprites and brilliant scrolling effects with each stage jam packed with baddies to eliminate. The soundtrack whilst not quite up to the 16 bit standard is still among the very best available on The Game Gear and best of all despite the Console only having 2 useable buttons almost all of the special moves have made it into this game.

There are sadly a few negatives namely the omission of my favourite character Max Thunder (who is a Pro Wrestler) and the fact that 2 stages had to be removed due to size limitations of the cartridge which takes the total stages down from 8 to just 6.

That aside Streets of Rage 2 on Game Gear is still a total classic and I would recommend it to any one with even a passing interest in this genre.

Vampire: Master of Darkness

Unlike all the other games on my list thus far Vampire: Master of Darkness was not actually a conversion of a Mega Drive game but was instead an original release for The Game Gear which was later ported over to The Master System.

The game is actually very similar to the all time classic Castlevania series involving the player taking on and eventually defeating the evil Dracula.

Just like the Castlevania series Vampire: Master of Darkness is an action platformer with levels scrolling from mainly left to right. All manner of baddies were thrown at the player including mad dogs, wolves, baseball bat wielding maniacs, skeletons, poltergeists and even an appearance by infamous serial killer Jack the Ripper.

Graphically the game was superb for the time period as was the excellent creepy sound track, the gameplay was classic Castlevania but best of all was the rather unique brooding and foreboding atmosphere that was pretty common on Home Consoles but less so on Handheld Consoles.

Any negatives? Not much to be honest maybe the pace of the game is a little slow especially near the start but to be honest I am really nit picking here.

If you are a fan of this genre you must try this game, although not quite in the same class as Castlevania it is still for me a classic!

Ristar

Originally released on The Sega Megadrive in 1995 and later ported over to Game Gear Ristar was a charming 2d Platforming game very much in the style of Sonic The Hedgehog.

The main character Ristar is apparently an anthropomorphic creature who is fighting against an evil space pirate called Kaiser Greedy.

Kaiser Greedy is attempting to control an entire planet via mind control and on top of that he has also kidnapped Ristar's father!

The gameplay is classic Sonic arcade style platforming with Ristar using his large and stretchable arms to reach high platforms as well as eliminating the bad guys. The pace of the game is considerably slower than Sonic The Hedgehog but has an increased focus on strategy.

Whilst the gameplay in this version is nearly identical to The Megadrive game the levels actually differ greatly probably due to the limitations of the hardware (such as less bad guys and several sections being removed from certain levels).

The only downside with Ristar is how short the game is, indeed the game can be completed in a single afternoon (battery life permitting), that aside I would have no problem recommending Ristar to any fans of this genre. Sadly despite the game receiving excellent reviews and selling very well Ristar never actually received a sequel although the game has been rereleased on several retro compilations in recent years as well as being added to The Nintendo Switch Online Expansion Pack in 2021.

Honourable Mentions

Dynamite Headdy

Dynamite Headdy was yet another Megadrive Conversion but to be honest when the game is this good who cares?

Dynamite Headdy was created by Treasure who are best known for the superb run and gun title Gunstar Heroes but if anything Dynamite Headdy might be even better.

Graphically the game is superb with very colourful and detailed levels and some very impressive and well animated sprites, the soundtrack is also very good considering the humble sound chip on The Game Gear.

The main character uses his head to detachable head to kill bad guys (hence the name Dynamite Headdy), speaking of the bad guys they are very odd and very Japanese in style (especially the creepy looking teddy bears). Throughout the game Dynamite Headdy can collect special powerups which can give him special powers for a limited time only (such as the ability to actually suck in his enemies similar to Kirby).

If you are a fan of this genre you will find plenty to enjoy here and although Dynamite Headdy is not quite in the same class as Sonic The Hedgehog it is still one of the finest platform games available on this machine.

Star Wars Return of the Jedi

As I am not really much of a fan of the movies a Star Wars game has to be good for me to show interest in it and Star Wars Return of The Jedi on Game Gear is certainly good.

Unlike most other games on this platform Return of The Jedi was not actually a Megadrive conversion but surprisingly a Super Nintendo conversion instead.

The game is essentially a 2d platformer/run and gun (much like the classic Gunstar Heroes on The Megadrive), each level within the game is roughly based on locations from the hit 1980's movie of the same name.

The player takes control of several important protagonists from the series including Princess Leia, Hans Sol and Luke Skywalker on their epic quest to defeat the Evil Empire.

The graphics are remarkable and actually very similar to The Super Nintendo version, the soundtrack is of high quality and most importantly the control system works very well and without any noticeable input lag.

The level design throughout the game are stunning and some of the boss fights are immense (especially Jabba The Hutt) not to mention the Endor speeder bike chase section.

If you are a fan of the Star Wars movies or just a fan of the genre you must check this game out!

The Jungle Book

Released in late 1994 The Jungle Book was an exceptionally good 2d platformer based on the legendary Disney animated movie.

Taking control of Mowgli (a young lad who was raised by Wolves) the player must flee from the evil Tiger Shere Khan. The plot involves Mowgli fleeing the jungle and attempting to reach the safety of his village, on his journey he receives help from several colourful characters including Baloo The Bear and Bagheera (who is a Panther).

There is much for platform fans to enjoy here including super graphics which are nearing on a par with the 16 bit home versions of the game, a legendary soundtrack full of Disney goodness and best of all classic old skool gameplay mainly involving Mowgli collecting various gems and fighting off bad guys by throwing bananas at them!

During this era there were a great many superb Disney platform games released on Sega platforms and The Jungle Book was right up there with the very best of them, if you like games from this genre you will love this.

Shinobi 2: The Silent Fury

Released in early 1993 Shinobi 2: The Silent Fury was a high class scrolling fighting game that was actually not a conversion from The Megadrive but instead an entirely new game made especially for The Game Gear.

The plot is very simple an evil group known as The Techo Warriors have taken over Neon City with the help of The Black Ninja (who is apparently a master ninja), so it is up to the player using Joe Musashi (who is luckily also a master ninja) to bring them to justice.

Graphically the game was superb with large character sprites and very detailed and smooth scrolling backgrounds. The soundtrack was also excellent bearing in mind the limitations of the Game Gear and most importantly the gameplay was spot on just as much fun as the home console versions of the day.

The only problem with Shinobi 2: The Silent Fury was the difficulty level, whilst I love a challenge the gameplay was for me too difficult but at least it did offer the players a password system in order to effectively save their progress.

All in all I would happily recommend this game to any fans of this series in fact try it even if your not a fan as it just may convert you!

Sonic Chaos

Sonic Chaos was released on both Game Gear and Master System in late 1993 and is often regarded as an unofficial sequel to the classic platformer Sonic The Hedgehog 2.

If you are a fan of Sonic or indeed a fan of this genre you are in for a real treat here as Sonic Chaos has everything you could want from a platform games.

Firstly the graphics are lovely even better than the earlier sonic games and very nearly on a par with the legendary Megadrive games. The soundtrack is classic Sonic and whilst not quite up the sky high standards of the 16 bit versions is still pretty striking and very best of all that tried and tested classic Sonic gameplay is fully intact.

Any negatives? Well perhaps the game is a little too easy (especially on some of the early levels) although to be fair Sonic The Hedgehog games have never been overly tough anyway.

That minor criticism aside Sonic Chaos was a wonderful game and fans of The Blue Blur will have hours of fun here.

Nintendo Game Boy Advance

Released in Europe in July 2001 The Game Boy Advance was the true next gen follow up to the all conquering Gameboy (released way back in 1989).

Essentially a portable Super Nintendo The Game Boy Advance (or GBA) received a number of high quality conversions from the 16 bit wonder as a result but also had a very impressive library of exclusive games which made the machine a must buy for all Nintendo fans.

The Game Boy Advance had a very impressive for the time period 32 bit processor, a large and colourful screen and even had shoulder buttons on the Console itself (similar in style to The Super Nintendo control pads).

Despite the increase in power the GBA had a superb battery life with a pair of AA batteries lasting up to 15 hours.

The only fly in the ointment here was the lack of a back light screen, this meant that on occasion it could be hard to see what was going on without some sort of direct light, this was eventually fixed however with the launch of The Game Boy Advance SP in 2003 which came complete with a front lit LCD screen. The SP version of The GBA would also come complete with a built in rechargeable battery eliminating the need for AA batteries and would actually be half the size of the older model due to its brand new 'Clam Shell' design.

The Game Boy Advance would go on to sell a phenomenal 81 million units around the world with a massive games library of well in excess of 800 releases. I will now attempt to pick my favourite 5 games and another 5 honourable mentions.

Top 5 Game Boy Advance Games

F Zero: Maximum Velocity

Released alongside The Game Boy Advance Console in Europe on 22 June 2001 F Zero: Maximum Velocity was a futuristic racing game based on the classic Super Nintendo game from 1990 F Zero.

F Zero: Maximum Velocity was the 3rd game in the series to date but actually the first ever F Zero game to appear on a handheld console.

The basic gameplay is very similar to the Super Nintendo original with the player controlling a futuristic hovercraft racing around an equally futuristic track against a variety of dangerous opponents.

Graphically the game was superb with stunning tracks and amazing animations with no hint of slowdown or glitching at all. Being an F Zero game it can be taken as read that the soundtrack was also of high quality.

The best feature of F Zero: Maximum Velocity was the added addition of a multiplayer mode and incredibly 2 players can player against each other with only a single cartridge required (although to be fair a Game Boy Advance link cable would be needed). This was very welcome at the time as the original Super Nintendo game had no multiplayer options at all.

F Zero: Maximum Velocity was for me one of the very best racing games ever released on handheld console, such was its popularity F Zero: Maximum Velocity was later rereleased on Nintendo Wii U via The Virtual Console back in 2014.

Advance Wars

Released in Europe around January of 2002 Advance Wars was a superb turn-based strategy game created by Intelligent Systems.

When I saw a preview for Advance Wars in an issue of Gamesmaster magazine I was really excited as games from this genre are generally only released on PC and so to play such a title on a handheld machine would be epic! Alas I was not disappointed.

The plot is very simple involving two warring factions (Blue Moon and Orange Star) fighting it out, the fighting eventually escalates to a World War and ends up involving several other factions including Green Earth and Yellow Comet.

The gameplay in Advance Wars is both fun and easy to understand, basically each mission consists of the player controlling one army and the CPU the other. There are only 2 ways to finish each mission and that is to either destroy your opponents entire army or even capture their base.

There are a huge amount of different military units to choose from and an excellent range of different maps to battle on each with its very own unique terrain and elevation.

In addition to the superb single player campaign multiplayer is also available in 2 different flavours. Firstly the standard VS Mode whereby 2 players battle each other using just 1 Game Boy Advance console and Link Mode which is largely the same except 2 separate machines are used and connected via the Game Boy Advance Link cable.

Advance Wars would go on to sell very well across the world resulting in several sequels including the excellent Battalion Wars on Gamecube in 2005 and more recently in 2023 Advance Wars 1+2 Re-Boot Camp on Nintendo Switch (essentially a high quality remake of the first 2 games).

If you are a fan of this genre you simply must try this game!

Sonic Advance

A Sonic The Hedgehog game appearing on a Nintendo Console? Surely a mistake! At least that is what I would have said a few years earlier but sadly after the Dreamcast was discontinued in early 2001

Sega had no choice but to exit The Hardware business and focus solely on creating software for other platforms including The Game Boy Advance.

Released in March of 2002 Sonic Advance was a fantastic 2d platformer starring The Blue Blur, clearly inspired by the decade old Megadrive titles this game was a dream for platform fans.

Graphically the game was lovely with large and well animated sprites and hugely detailed levels, the soundtrack was classic Sega with several very catchy tunes and best of all the gameplay was brilliant.

In addition to Sonic the player can also choose to play as Tails, Knuckles or Amy Rose. Each character has their own strengths and weaknesses which can really affect the feel of the game which helps to add much needed variety to the gameplay.

Whilst not quite in the same league as the seminal Megadrive games Sonic Advance is still a high quality platformer which all fans of this genre will love.

Mario Kart Super Circuit

As a huge fan of the Mario Kart series I was extremely excited for the release of Mario Kart Super Circuit on Game Boy Advance.

The game was originally intended to be a launch title for The Game Boy Advance in Europe around June 2001 but sadly the game was slightly delayed until September of 2001 but boy was it worth the extra wait!

Firstly the game has superb graphics which are in my opinion even better than the original Super Nintendo game, each of the 8 different characters look amazing and are very well animated whilst the tracks look superb with astounding 'Mode 7' style rotational effects. Speaking of the tracks Mario Kart Super Circuit offers 40 of them, including for the first time in the series tracks from earlier Mario Kart titles.

Mario Kart Super Circuit offered plenty of modes for the single player including a Quick Run option, a Time Trial mode and best of all a Gran Prix mode. In the Gran Prix mode the player has to compete in various Cup competitions in order to unlock hidden tracks and items, this mode added real longevity to the single player game.

But wait the fun does not stop there as Mario Kart Super Circuit also offered Multiplayer, in this mode up to 4 human players can compete against each other in both Racing and Battle modes.

The game offers several different set up options in Multiplayer including the ability to play with 4 human players using just a single cartridge (although to be fair there are some limitations here including the ability to only select a single racer and just a handful of tracks).

Mario Kart Super Circuit is without question the best racing game ever made for The Game Boy Advance and in my opinion it is one of the greatest racing games on any format.

Such was the games huge popularity that it has recently been made available on The Nintendo Switch via the + Expansion Pack subscription service. Whether you play Mario Kart Super Circuit on Game Boy Advance or via Nintendo Switch you will not be disappointed a must play for any Nintendo fans.

Metroid Fusion

Released in late 2002 in Europe Metroid Fusion was a superb action/adventure game with some puzzle solving elements.

Metroid Fusion is actually very similar to the legendary Super Nintendo game Super Metroid (which is no bad thing), just like the earlier games in this series the protagonist here is Samus Arun (who is a female bounty hunter).

In Metroid Fusion Samus Arun is tasked with destroying a planet that has become infected with a nasty parasitic organism known as X.

Graphically Metroid Fusion is amazing with incredibly large and well detailed levels and a great many of the enemy sprites are huge and very well animated. The soundtrack is outstanding as you would probably expect from a game in this brilliant series.

Whilst the gameplay will be very familiar to anybody who played the earlier titles Metroid Fusion does offer a few new additions to the gameplay notably Samus having the added ability to transform into a tiny ball in order to gain access to otherwise restricted areas.

Any negatives? Well only that towards the end of the game Metroid Fusion really ramps up the difficulty rather quickly, although to be fair the earlier Metroid games are also very tough so I suppose fans of the series will be used to that.

Metroid Fusion is one of the best games on The Game Boy Advance and if you are a fan of this genre then it really is a must own game.

Honourable Mentions

Doom

Based on the classic PC game of the same name Doom was converted onto The Game Boy Advance in late 2001 and whilst not quite up to the same standard as some of the other versions of Doom it still packed quite a punch!

The graphics on this version were very impressive and were very nearly on par with the PC version of Doom, the soundtrack was also very decent bearing in mind the technical limitations of the Game Boy Advance sound chip.

Best of all the gameplay for which the Doom was so renown for is here in abundance and the overall performance of the game was highly impressive with very little in the way of noticeable slowdown.

In addition to single player levels Doom on Game Boy Advance also offered a limited Multiplayer mode with 8 deathmatch maps being made available to the player (although a Game Boy Advance link cable was required for this mode).

Sadly there were a few compromises made to get Doom across to Game Boy Advance namely several enemy types had to be removed due to space limitations of the cartridge format, as a result of this there are no Spider demons or Cyber demons in this version).

That aside Doom on Game Boy Advance is still a fantastic game in its own right and fans of the series will no doubt have lots of fun here.

Super Mario Advance 2: Super Mario World

Released in April of 2002 in Europe Super Mario Advance 2 was a high quality conversion of The Super Nintendo classic Super Mario World.

Just like the Super Nintendo original Super Mario Advance 2 contains 96 levels full of superlative 2d platforming gameplay.

Graphically the game was nearly identical to its 16 bit cousin and probably the best graphics seen up to this point on The Game Boy Advance. Due to the lack of buttons available on The Game Boy Advance compared to The Super Nintendo joypad the control system was slightly changed but to be honest after a few minutes it really becomes second nature.

Sadly one or two features of Super Mario World had to be cut due to the limitations of the handheld machine including the omission of the two player mode. For me this really does hurt the game and that is the main reason why it does not appear in my Top 5 Game Boy Advance games.

Despite this drawback Super Mario Advance 2 was still a top draw conversion and a game I would happily recommend to Nintendo fans.

This version of Super Mario World has been rereleased several times over the years including on The Nintendo Wii U in 2016 via the Virtual Console and very recently as part of the Nintendo Switch + Expansion Pack on The Nintendo Switch.

Castlevania: Aria of Sorrow

As a huge fan of the series I was really looking forward to the release of a Castlevania game on The Game Boy Advance and in the end we ended up getting 3 of them!

The game I eventually choose to cover was the final game in this trilogy entitled Castlevania: Aria of Sorrow (released in 2003).

Just like the majority of the other games in this classic franchise Castlevania: Aria of Sorrow was a high class action and adventure title.

The plot here involves the Belmont clan (a well respected family of Vampire hunters) once again taking on the evil Dracula but this time in the future (around the year 2035). Bizarrely despite the game being set well into the future most of the available weaponry is still Medieval based (axes, spears and swords mostly) so fans of the earlier games in the Castlevania series will still feel at home here.

Graphically the game was superb with incredibly well animated and large sprites and some excellent and quite imaginative level designs. I have to say however that the soundtrack was for whatever reason not really up to the standard of the earlier Castlevania titles (especially the all time classic Super Nintendo hit Castlevania: Symphony of the Night).

That minor quibble aside I would still recommend Castlevania:Aria of Sorrow to any fans of this genre it is simply the best game of its kind on Game Boy Advance.

Crash Bandicoot 2: N-Tranced

I really enjoyed playing Crash Bandicoot on Playstation in the late 1990s and so this version for the Game Boy Advance was right up my street.

Released in early 2003 Crash Bandicoot 2: N-Tranced was the second game in the series made for Game Boy Advance and the eight game in the series overall.

The plot here involves Crash Bandicoot attempting to save his friend Crunch and his little sister Cocu from the evil clutches of Doctor N Tropy (who has apparently hypnotized them into helping him conquer the universe).

The game actually plays very similar to those earlier Playstation games which is no bad thing at all, the controls are easy to pick up and very responsive, the graphics whilst not in the same league as The Playstation games are still very impressive (especially the 3D stages featuring Cocu Bandicoot) and the sound is very cheerful as well.

The single player game was very big for the time period with over 30 levels for Crash to conquer with each level getting a touch more difficult until the final battle with Doctor N Tropy.

Any negatives? Nothing really except maybe Crash Bandicoot 2: N-Tranced does not really offer the player anything new but having said that when the game is this much fun who cares?

Mario vs Donkey Kong

Released in 2004 Mario vs Donkey Kong was a puzzle platforming game featuring 2 of the most iconic characters in videogame history Super Mario and Donkey Kong.

These 2 titans of gaming originally clashed in the 1981 classic arcade game entitled Donkey Kong and over 20 years later the 2 have obviously not yet buried the hatchet!

The plot was quite unique for the time period rather than Princess Peach being kidnapped again here Donkey Kong becomes angry when he is unable to buy a certain wind up toy, so angry is the massive guerrilla that he breaks into a toy factory owned by Mario and steals all his toys which results in the 2 legends squaring off.

The gameplay in Mario vs Donkey Kong consists of platform sections which will be very familiar to fans of The Super Mario series but also has elements of puzzle solving (such as Mario needing to find a certain key in order to progress to the next level). A great many of the levels here are clearly based on the original Game Boy classic Donkey Kong (released in 1994) with similar level design and pacing.

Whilst Mario vs Donkey Kong could not really compete with some of the other Super Mario games of this era it was still very popular and went on to sell well over 1 million copies.

I would encourage any fans of this genre or any fans of either Super Mario or Donkey Kong to try this game, you will not be disappointed.

Sony PSP

Released in Europe on 1 September 2005 The PSP (Playstation Portable) was Sony's first ever attempt at making a handheld console.

At the time of its release The PSP was far more powerful than any other handheld console on the market, in fact it was powerful that it was nearly a match for Sony's all conquering home console The Playstation 2 (as a result of this The PSP received numerous high class conversions from said console).

The PSP boasted very advanced 3d visuals, basic web browsing and of course multimedia playback, the software came on a small disc based format named UMD. A standard UMD could hold up to an astonishing 1.8GB of data (compared to just 64mbof storage on a standard cartridge for Nintendo's DS console).

As a result of this PSP games were generally more sophisticated than most other handheld games due to the amount of content that could be added (such as cut scenes and voice acting).

There were several drawbacks however to using UMD's as a storage medium namely whereas cartridges on Nintendo DS could load up within a few seconds a PSP title would generally take over a minute, this would not be a problem on a home console but it is not really good enough on a handheld machine (especially if for example you were just trying to pass a few minutes on a bus trip for example).

The other issue with UMD's is the lack of storage to actually save your gaming progress, as a result PSP owners needed to buy an internal memory card in order to actually save their progress (at the time of the PSP's release these memory cards were very pricey and actually very difficult to even find).

Another problem with The PSP was the slightly disappointing battery life, at a push you could probably get around 6 hours compared to over 20 hours on a Nintendo DS, this severally weakened the appeal of the console in my opinion.

Despite the drawbacks The PSP would be very successful indeed selling in excess of 80 million units making it the most successful handheld console ever that was not manufactured by Nintendo.

Whilst The PSP does not have a library as large as either The Game Boy Advance or The DS it still had over 600 games and so to pick just 5 of my favourites and 5 more honourable mentions will be tough, so here goes.

Top 5 PSP Games

Gran Turismo PSP

Released in late 2009 Gran Turismo on The PSP was a top class driving simulator based upon the legendary Playstation series of the same name.

The gameplay here is classic Gran Turismo with realistic handling and dynamo racing physics, graphically the game was really special (roughly equivalent to the superb Gran Turismo 4 on Playstation 2) and the sound effects were also very impressive (in particular the engine noises were very true to life).

Whereas other racing games on The PSP would offer only a handful of different tracks and vehicles Gran Turismo PSP had a mammoth 45 tracks and a gargantuan 833 vehicles (yes 833).

The player had much to do here with Gran Turismo PSP offering Single Races, Time Trials and Drift trials, in addition to these modes Gran Turismo also had various Driving Missions. When the Driving Missions were completed the player would be rewarded with both extra tracks and vehicles.

Any negatives? Well the only thing really and it is a common problem on this platform loading times, Gran Turismo PSP seems to take an age to initially load up and then takes about 45 seconds to load up each track from the main menu which can be very annoying if you are pushed for time.

That aside Gran Turismo PSP was a stunning title and for me the very best racing game on the console.

Killzone Liberation

Killzone Liberation was released in November of 2006 and was an excellent first person shooter based upon the very impressive Killzone series which debuted a few years earlier on The Playstation 2.

The plot here centres around a fictional futuristic world in the aftermath of a nuclear war, the player takes on the role of a soldier within the ISA (Interplanetary Strategic Alliance) fighting against the Helghast (a group of Genetically Mutated Super Soldiers).

Killzone Liberation has much to admire including superb graphics (even better than the original Playstation 2 game for me), a moody and atmospheric soundtrack and extremely easy to pick up and play old skool gameplay.

Killzone Liberation features an excellent single player campaign for the player to sink their teeth into and even more impressive features an excellent multiplayer mode as well. In multiplayer mode the player can choose to take part in several different gameplay modes including Deathmatch (here it is simply every man for himself shoot anybody that moves), Team Deathmatch (where one team must eliminate the other) and also Capture The Flag (this involves each team attempting to steal the flag of their enemies and return it to their base).

Generally first person shooters do not work on handheld consoles but in the case of Killzone Liberation it really did, sadly this series has largely disappeared now as the most recent entry was way back in 2013 (Killzone Shadow Fall on Playstation 4). Fingers crossed for a remaster at some stage!

Capcom Classics Remixed

As a huge fan of retro gaming I have always been very fond of retro game compilations and for me this collection of titles called Capcom Classics Remixed is arguably the best ever assembled on a handheld console.

There are a grand total of 20 games from yesteryear including so many stone wall classics including legendary scrolling beat em up Final Fight (1991), amazing hack and slash them up Strider (1989) and seminal scrolling shoot em up Forgotten Worlds (1988).

Each game was more or less arcade perfect and to make things even better Capcom Classics Remixed offers so much extra content for the player including unlockable art works, music tracks and a brief history of each game and its franchise.

Any negatives? Well a version of Street Fighter 2 would have been welcome (especially Turbo) but that aside this is a fantastic retro collection and it is probably my most played PSP game of all time.

Virtua Tennis World Tour

Released in September of 2005 alongside The PSP console in Europe Virtua Tennis World Tour was a superb arcade style tennis game from Sega.

The basic gameplay was almost identical to the Dreamcast and Playstation 2 versions (no bad thing as they were among the very best tennis games ever created).

Graphically the game was remarkable for a handheld title especially considering this was a launch title (in fact the graphics were for me even better than Virtua Tennis 2 on Playstation 2). The sprites looked fantastic huge and very well animated and the courts looked brilliant with very realistic looking crowd members. The sound effects of the ball were also spot on (I especially loved the way the ball sounds when it bounces on different surfaces such as clay).

Virtua Tennis World Tour offered the player many different game modes including Quick Matches, Exhibition Matches, Ball Games, Tournament Mode and of courses a World Tour Mode.

The World Tour Mode is essentially a Career Mode of sorts with the player completing training exercises and winning Tournaments in order to unlock more players and courts.

There was even a Multiplayer Mode available for up to 4 human players, this was done via The PSP's Wi Fi features (I tried this at the time of release and whilst it did not always work when it did it was hugely entertaining with no lag at all).

If you are a fan of tennis games or just a fan of sports titles in general you simply must try this game, in my opinion it is by far the best ever tennis game available on any handheld machine.

Ridge Racer

Another launch title for The PSP in Europe Ridge Racer was a stunning arcade style racer based on the earlier hit Playstation and Arcade games.

The basic gameplay was identical to the earlier Playstation 1 and 2 games with over the top power sliding and high speed thrills very much being the order of the day!

Ridge Racer on The PSP was essentially a high class compilation containing all the very best cars and tracks from the entire series, 58 cars were available to the player (although to be fair a great many needed to be unlocked) and 12 courses (10 of which were from earlier Ridge Racer games and 2 were completely new and exclusive to this version).

Graphically the game was superb and easily a match for Ridge Racer 5 on Playstation 2, the soundtrack was banging with many memorable tunes and best of all the controls were responsive and very easily to pick up.

Back in the day it became customary for any new Sony machine to be launched with a new version of Ridge Racer, this occurred with The Playstation 1 (Ridge Racer), Playstation 2 (Ridge Racer 5), PSP (Ridge Racer PSP) and finally Playstation 3 (Ridge Racer 7).

Sadly like most good things in gaming it is no longer the case.

If you are a fan of arcade style racing you must try this as it is quite simply one of the very best available on any console.

Honourable Mentions

Wipeout Pure

I have always been a fan of The Wipeout series ever since I played it in a branch of Comet's around 1996, I eventually owned all 3 Wipeout games on The Original Playstation and Wipeout Fusion on The Playstation 2.

With this in mind I was really looking forward to playing this version on PSP entitled Wipeout Pure.

The first thing that really hit me with Wipeout Pure was how stunning the graphics were (in my opinion they were even better than Wipeout Fusion on Playstation 2). Not only were the graphics absolutely stunning but the speed at which the game moved was breakneck (with no hint of slowdown or clipping).

The Soundtrack was predicably excellent (no surprise given the series history of excellent Electronica tunes) and best of all the gameplay was classic Wipeout! Despite the incredible speed of the game the control system was able to keep up with no input lag at all.

Any downers? Well like some of the earlier games in the series maybe Wipeout Pure is at times just a little too difficult. This is especially the case on some of the later courses which can be devilishly hard to navigate.

That aside I would recommend Wipeout Pure to any fans of the series or any fans of racing games in general, a real class act!

Powerstone Collection

The first 2 Powerstone games were superb and rather madcap arena based beat em up's with the added bonus of using various weaponry. Both games were originally released as Arcade Cabinets and ported over perfectly to The Sega Dreamcast.

Sadly despite the series immense popularity there were to be no more Powerstone games, but at the very least we do have Powerstone Collection on PSP to fall back on.

Essentially Powerstone Collection on PSP is a high quality compilation of both Powerstone and Powerstone 2 with the added bonus of new content made specially for this version.

The new content included 12 new items to use in combat (mainly new weapons) and the added ability to play as previously locked characters including Kraken (an evil pirate captain), Valgas (a former soldier) and Gourmand (a crazy chef).

If you have any interest in this genre you simply must play Powerstone Collection on PSP, for me it is the very best beat em up available on the console.

Gradius Collection

For the most part I do not play many 2d scrolling shooters as I find them far too difficult but I have always enjoyed The Gradius series and with that in mind this particular title is right up my street.

Gradius Collection on PSP is a compilation featuring 5 spot on conversions from various Arcade Cabinet from the late 1980's and early 1990's (they include Gradius, Gradius 2: Gofer No Yaber, Gradius 3, Gradius Gaiden and Gradius 4).

Unusually for a compilation every single game here is a stone wall classic! Most of the time there would be at least 1 average game to pad the collection out but not here.

The basic gameplay for Gradius involves the player controlling a tiny spacecraft fighting an ever increasing wave of nasties, as the player progresses they will gain access to new and improved weaponry.

Graphically all the games here are quite striking despite their age whilst each Gradius title includes some superb music scores throughout.

Even better for me none of these games are too difficult meaning that even I can complete them (eventually).

All in all if you are a fan of this genre you simply must try Gradius Collection, I promise you will love it!

LocoRoco

Released in 2006 LocoRoco was a very original 2d platformer developed by Japan Studio (an internal Sony owner studio based in Tokyo).

LocoRoco differs from a great many other games in this genre due to the unique control system, here the player has to rotate the gaming environment by pressing The PSP's shoulder buttons.

Doing this helps the main character (who is made of jelly) to safely travel through each level whilst avoiding various traps and nasties.

The graphics in LocoRoco whilst certainly not state of the art were very bright and colourful (like a through back to the 16 bit era), the soundtrack was also impressive with very mellow tunes complimenting the gameplay immensely.

LocoRoco although not really a big commercial success it did sell enough copies to receive several sequels and even a 2017 Remaster on Playstation 4.

Whilst not really in the same league as Super Mario or Sonic The Hedgehog LocoRoco still has much to offer for fans of 2d platform games, just don't go into it thinking it will change your life!

Daxter

Released in 2006 Daxter was an awesome 3d platform game based upon the legendary Playstation 2 series Jak and Daxter.

This game has so much for fans of the genre to enjoy including some of the very best graphics yet seen on The PSP, some brilliant music scores, amazingly well thought out level designs and a very easy to pick up and play control system.

Unlike many other games from this era Daxter also has some real laugh out loud moments to enjoy as well (this was in stark contrast to the earlier Playstation 2 games which by the end of the series were pretty dark in content).

The plot involved Daxter rescuing his old friend Jak from the clutches of the evil Krimzon Guard (a sort of Military Police unit). The voice acting for the time was really a cut above most other efforts and it really helped draw me into the story.

Any negatives? Well as per usual with The PSP some of the loading times are very long, this can at times really take you out of the moment.

That aside I would have no hesitation recommending Daxter to any PSP owners out there, it is simply the best 3d platformer available on the machine.

Nintendo Dual Screen (DS)

Following on from the massively successful Game Boy Advance console Nintendo would go on to release The Dual Screen (or simply DS for short) in Europe during March 2005.

The Nintendo DS was a very original product as it had a very unusual Touch-Screen design (via a stylus pen). This rather open design style helped to broaden the horizons of the console to include not just gamers but the more casual consumer as well (hence the DS games library including a great many titles that would not usually appeal to gamers but sold very well such as Brain Training or Nintendogs).

Although not anywhere near as powerful as The Sony PSP in every other aspect The Nintendo DS was the king due to having a far larger and higher quality library of games, much better battery life performance, far quicker loading times (thanks mainly to The DS still using cartridges) and of course was far cheaper to purchase at retail.

The DS was also backwards compatible with all Game Boy Advance games (giving the console an extra 800 + games to choose from). Over the years there were several revisions to the hardware namely The Nintendo DS Lite. The DS Lite was a lighter, slimmer model of the original DS with further improved battery life and a brighter screen.

Incredibly The Nintendo DS would go on to sell well in excess of 150 million units over its lifetime making it the most successful Nintendo console of all time and second most successful overall behind only the legendary Sony Playstation 2.

The DS had a huge library of high quality games (indeed there were over 3000 titles to choose from). So to pick just 5 favourites and 5 more honourable mentions will not be easy but I look forward to the challenge I hope you will join me.

Mario Kart DS

Released in November 2005 Mario Kart DS was the fifth game in the legendary series and in my opinion one of the very best.

There are several reasons as to why I love this game so much including the fact that in some respects Mario Kart DS is almost a compilation of all the classic older games in the series in that it features a great many of the very best tracks from The Super Nintendo, Nintendo 64, Game Boy Advance and Gamecube versions of the game (including my personal favourite track Rainbow Road from The Super Nintendo).

 In total there are 32 tracks to race on (16 classic tracks and 16 brand new original tracks) with each one offering a unique challenge.

Graphically the game was superb for the time and for me was nearly as good looking as Mario Kart: Double Dash on Gamecube. Mario Kart DS is so bright and vivid with amazingly well animated racers and very impressive trackside detail. Speaking of the racers there are a total of 12 to choose from including old favourites such as Super Mario, Luigi and Bowser and newcomers to the series such as Dry Bones. Just like the earlier games in the series each selectable character has his or her own strengths and weaknesses (I usually pick Yoshi).

In addition to a fantastic one player mode (including Single Races, Gran Prix, Mission Mode and Time Trial) Mario Kart DS offered a superb multiplayer mode. Around this time I worked at Game and during my lunch hour myself and several other members of staff would race against each other via The Nintendo Wi Fi Connection (meaning 4 human players can race against each other so long as they are within a short distance of each other). Sadly this service was withdrawn in 2014 but whilst it lasted it really was incredible.

All in all I would recommend Mario Kart DS to anybody as for me it is not only the best racing game on the platform but maybe the best game on The DS period!

The Legend of Zelda: The Phantom Hourglass

Despite not really being a big fan of this genre I have always enjoyed The Legend of Zelda games and that includes this fine effort The Phantom Hourglass released for The Nintendo DS in late 2007.

The Phantom Hourglass was a sequel to the often underrated Gamecube title The Legend of Zelda: The Wind Waker.

Just like the Gamecube title The Phantom Hourglass had very impressive for the time period 3D Cel- Shaded graphics viewed from the usual overhead camera viewpoint.

Most of the action here takes place on the open seas with Link piloting a boat travelling around various Islands attempting to find

Princess Zelda who has been kidnapped and being held aboard a terrifying ghost ship.

The gameplay here is very much classic The Legend of Zelda with much exploring and puzzle solving to be done mixed in with the occasional battle.

One area where The Phantom Hourglass is an improvement over previous titles in this series is in the humour of the game. Some of the earlier titles (especially Majora's Mask on Nintendo 64) had rather a dark foreboding atmosphere whereas here the game has a much cheerier nature similar to the earlier games in the series (such as my favourite Link To The Past on Super Nintendo).

Whilst The Phantom Hourglass is not the best game in the series it still has much to offer fans of this genre. The game was later released on Nintendo Wi U via the Virtual Console in late 2015, this version of The phantom Hourglass was improved further thanks to the added bonus of using The Nintendo Wi U touchscreen controller.

Tetris DS

I spend many a happy hour playing Tetris on The Nintendo Gameboy back in the early 1990's and so I was very happy to see the release of Tetris DS during the spring of 2006.

The basic gameplay of Tetris DS was largely the same as the earlier games namely blocks of different sizes and shapes fall down the screen, the player must then quickly use the falling pieces (called Tetrominoes) to create Horizontal lines. When this is done correctly the completed line will disappear with the next pieces falling down to the next level as a direct result.

Players will be rewarded for achieving this with points which then directly leads to an increase in difficulty, eventually even the very best players will be overcome resulting in 'Game Over'.

Tetris DS did have some improvements over the earlier Gameboy title including much improved graphics (and in full colour of course), much improved controls due to the to the touch screen and best of all the addition of an excellent multiplayer mode (via Nintendo's Wi FI Connection) up to 4 players could play head to head as long as they were in close proximity.

All in all Tetris is for me the best puzzle game on the Nintendo DS and is a must own for fans of the series.

New Super Mario Bros

Released during the summer of 2006 New Super Mario Bros was actually the first new 2d platform game in the legendary series since the glory days of The Super Nintendo.

The gameplay here is classic Super Mario with the vast majority of levels moving from left to right and ending with Mario (or indeed his underrated brother Luigi) overcoming a series of obstacles and baddies in order to reach the flagpole located at the levels end.

Unlike earlier games in the 2d series however here Mario can make use of several skills which were formerly exclusive to his 3d adventures (such as the ability to triple jump, wall jump and ground pound).

The graphics are also brand new in that whilst the gameplay does indeed take place over a 2d plane the actual sprites and objects located in each level are rendered in 3d making for an almost pop up book style of artwork (very nicely done).

New Super Mario Bros was a huge adventure containing well over 80 levels spread over 8 totally unique worlds, the game also offered an excellent Multiplayer Mode whereby 2 human player's could play against each other over 5 different levels (as either Mario or Luigi) in order to see who could obtain a preset number of stars first.

New Super Mario Bros also featured a large number of Minigames to play through many of which were actually carried over from Super Mario 64 DS, this greatly increased the longevity of the game.

New Super Mario Bros would go on to sell an unbelievable 30 Million copies making it by some distance the best selling game on The Nintendo DS and one of the very best selling games of all time.

If you are a fan of this series or of this genre you simply must try this game as it is for me the best platformer game available on any portable system period!

Phoenix Wright: Ace Attorney

Released in the spring of 2006 Phoenix Wright: Ace Attorney was a visual adventure game which usually would be more at home on a home Computer, however due to the unique touchscreen controls of The Nintendo DS the game actually works really well on a handheld machine.

The player assumes the role of the aforementioned Phoenix Wright who must successfully defend various clients against charges of murder (there are I believe 5 different cases in total).

The gameplay in Phoenix Wright: Ace Attorney is mainly split into 2 parts which are Investigations and Courtroom Trials.

The investigation part of the game takes place before the actual trial and involves the player talking to various people (including witnesses, police officers and of course clients) and examining various pieces of evidence.

Whilst during the Courtroom Trial part of the game the player can attempt to cross examine various witnesses in order to uncover any inconsistencies or lies in their testimonies. If the player can successfully solve a case and get their client off the hook the next case opens up for them.

Although I have no wish to return to the game once I had finished it I would still recommend Phoenix Wright: Ace Attorney to any DS owners out there as there is very little else like it on the system.

There have been several new entries in this series since 2006 including the excellent Trials and Tribulations released on Nintendo Wii in 2010 but for me Ace Attorney is still my personal favourite.

Honourable Mentions

Diddy Kong Racing DS

Diddy Kong Racing was released on The Nintendo DS in early 2007, it was based upon the Nintendo 64 classic of the same name.

Sadly the original developers of the game Rare had since defected to Microsoft which meant that several of the main characters had to be removed due to licensing issues (including Banjo and Conker who were in turn replaced by Dixie Kong and Tiny Kong respectively).

That aside Diddy Kong Racing DS was an extremely impressive port of the Nintendo 64 classic with superb cartoony graphics, cheery and upbeat tunes and sound effects and a host of superbly designed and extremely attractive tracks.

The gameplay is similar to the early editions of Super Mario Kart with the added bonus of being able to use a whole host of different vehicles including Hovercrafts and even Planes.

Probably the only reason why I think Diddy Kong Racing DS falls just short of being a classic is due to the slightly spongy controls, on occasion there is a very slight input lag which just takes the shine off the game slightly (this is especially felt on some of the latter tougher tracks).

That aside Diddy Kong Racing DS is a high class racing game that fans of the genre should definitely check out.

Super Mario 64 DS

Released alongside The Nintendo DS in Europe in March 2005 Super Mario 64 DS was an excellent conversion of The Nintendo 64 classic.

The original Super Mario 64 was a stunning 3d platform game featuring Nintendo's mascot plumber. When I first saw footage of the game on an episode of Channel 4's Gamesmaster I honestly thought I was watching a cut scene but to my amazement it was the actual in game graphics.

The controls were sublime largely due to the superb Nintendo 64 Analogue controls and best of all Super Mario 64 had some of the most interesting and inventive levels ever seen up to this point.

The DS version actually manages to improve further on the original game in some respects namely with the added ability to play as more characters (including Yoshi, Wario and Luigi) and the added bonus of 30 extra stars to collect (now 150 up from 120 in the original game).

Sadly though it is not all good news as Super Mario 64 DS is somewhat lacking in the control department, this is in my opinion down to the lack of analogue controls on The DS compared to The Nintendo 64 controller. It took me ages to get used to the control system here which combines both the d pad and touch screen controls with somewhat mixed results.

That aside this is a very solid remake of a classic and is still a great example of how a 3d platformer should play even today.

Sonic Rush

I really loved Sonic The Hedgehog games on The Sega Megadrive during the early to mid 1990's but felt that soon afterwards Sonic lost his way with a series of somewhat average releases. Because of this I was a little bit sceptical about this game Sonic Rush (released in 2005).

However I soon realised on playing Sonic Rush that I was worrying needlessly as the game is really fun and in many ways a thrown back to the halcyon days of the Sega Megadrive.

Sonic Rush is so fast and so arcadey that fans of this genre will simply fall in love with it, graphically the game was superb with huge sprites that are both very colourful and well animated, the backdrops are lush with some of the best graphics seen on The Nintendo DS up to this point. Speaking of the graphics although the game is 2d platforming it has shades of 3d in that most of the boss characters, playable characters and selected special stages are rendered in 3d (giving the game a very unique 2.5d look). Also both screen are used on Sonic Rush with the player moving between them as they progress through the level, this really helps in my opinion as you can see far more of the level at any time which is handy when you are running through at such a frantic pace.

In addition to the excellent single player game Sonic Rush also offers a Multiplayer option whereby 2 players can compete head to head playing as either Sonic or Blaze (who is a cat) to see who can reach the end of the level first.

Any negatives? Well yes surprisingly the music in this game is extremely poor which is a surprise given how good the music was on the old Megadrive titles. Some of the voice overs are also of poor quality in my opinion.

No matter though Sonic Rush is still a high class platformer that fans of the blue blur will really appreciate.

Star Trek: Tactical Assault

As a big fan of Star Trek I have always enjoy videogames based on the franchise even though I do appreciate that to non fans they often seem like cynical cash grabs or dull space combat games.

To be fair that is probably true but putting that aside this game Star Trek: Tactical Assault released on Nintendo DS in late 2006 is a very enjoyable and easy to pick up and play space combat simulator.

In the single player mode you take control of a young officer who is commanding a small frigate and by completing various missions and gaining several promotions can progress onto commanding more advanced and powerful vessels.

This campaign was really fun but to be honest I spent most of my time playing the Random Battle mode where you can choose a starship of your choice (from as selection of around 20) and take on the cpu who is playing as an equivalent vessel usually from a different faction (including Klingons, Starfleet, Romulans and more). This mode was hugely entertaining and for me is even better than some of the PC space combat sims from the same era.

There was also a Multiplayer Mode where 2 humans can duel it out in a random battle although I have never tried this myself so I cannot comment on it.

All in all whilst it may not appeal to non fans if you are partial to a bit of Star Trek you could do far worse than picking up this fun little game.

Castlevania: Dawn of Sorrow

Being a big fan of this series (especially Super Castlevania 4 on Super Nintendo) I was really looking forward to this game and I was not to be disappointed.

Castlevania: Dawn of Sorrow was released in September of 2005 and like the majority of the other games in this legendary series it was an action adventure game played via a 2d perspective.

Both screens of The Nintendo DS are used here with the lower screen showing the action and the upper screen displaying a map. This really helped me during some of the more tricky moments as on the earlier titles I had to keep pausing the game to check out the map on the main menu but here there is no need to stop playing just simply have a gander at the top screen!

That aside this game plays just like the Super Nintendo game (clearly a good thing) with the player assuming the role of a vampire hunter who has to fight his way through hordes of demons and various other member of the undead (we have all been there).

Graphically the game was superb with large and well animated sprites and some terrific levels which really helped to bring the Castlevania universe to life. The sound was of high quality as was to be expected with rather macabre tunes playing throughout the game.

The only fault I could really find with this game was how short it was, usually for a Castlevania game as they usually take some time but here Dawn of Sorrow could be finished in around 4 to 5 hours which is a real shame.

Apart from that this game is perfect and is a joy to play through even now.

Well my friends we have finally reached the end if by some small chance you enjoyed this book (both of you) then you might want to check out my other books available on Amazon including Console Gaming in The 1990's and Arcade Gaming in The 1990's.

I also hope you will join me in the near future for my next book which will be regarding my 50 favourite Videogames of all time, thanks again.

Regards

Eric Bowden

Printed in Great Britain
by Amazon

31053381R00036